LAKE DISTRICT
WITH COLOURMASTER

LAKE DISTRICT

WITH COLOURMASTER

Published by Colourmaster International
Caxton Road, St Ives, Huntingdon, England

FIRST PUBLISHED 1972

PUBLISHED BY COLOURMASTER INTERNATIONAL
PRINTED IN GREAT BRITAIN BY PHOTO PRECISION LTD, ST IVES, HUNTINGDON
ISBN 0 85933 006 0

INTRODUCTION

Most of the Lake District is designated as a National Park, which means that its natural beauty is preserved for the pleasure of the public. Compactly situated in an area of only nine hundred square miles, it contains some magnificent scenery and even today it is still possible to find peace and tranquillity within its bounds. Austere but majestic craggy rock outcrops and bare mountain sides contrast with lush valley pastures; there are peat bogs and birch woods; bracken clad fells and tree covered islets; bubbling becks and dramatic cascades; deep-set lakes whose surfaces mirror their surroundings; dry-stone walls and pack-horse bridges; prehistoric stone circles and ancient earth-works; fifteen lakes and as many mountain passes; unbroken fell ponies and wild red deer; ravens and kestrels, lapwings and curlews; cotton-grass and daffodils, ferns and lobelia. These are some of the treasures in store for those visiting or returning to Lakeland.

The beginning of the popularity of the Lake District goes back to the nineteenth and indeed to the latter years of the eighteenth century when it became closely identified with such sensitive and brilliant writers of poetry and prose as Gray, Wordsworth, Coleridge, Southey, De Quincey, Ruskin and later, Sir Hugh Walpole. Its appeal, however, is by no means limited to writers in search of inspiration. Walkers and climbers, artists and photographers, naturalists and geologists are among the many specialists who find much to command their attention there but, additionally, there are the countless numbers of lovers of this glorious district who make no claim to being specialists but who dearly love to re-visit it whenever they can.

The colour and the black and white illustrations have been carefully selected to show something of the wonderfully varied views and vistas that the Lake District has to offer. The captions are deliberately brief and mainly factual in the belief that the pictures, very largely, can speak for themselves about one of the most beautiful parts of the British Isles. Easy of access by road and rail, the area includes England's highest mountains and her largest lakes, but it is the sheer diversity of the scenery that leaves such a lasting impression in the minds of those who are fortunate enough to have seen it for themselves.

Hawes Water and Harter Fell.

There is a fine, albeit sometimes strenuous walk from Howtown, which is halfway down the east side of Ullswater, to Hawes Water, in the course of which a good view is obtained from the high ridge which includes parts of both of the lakes. Hawes Water, over three miles long, is now a reservoir for the city of Manchester. Harter Fell, seen in the background of the photograph, is just over two thousand five hundred feet in height.

Coniston Water.

More than five miles long, Coniston becomes more and more attractive as one moves northwards towards the head of the lake, both sides of which are attractively wooded, as are its Peel and Fir Islands. Coniston village, in a charming setting below Yewdale Crags, is half a mile from the lake and makes an excellent centre from which to explore Ambleside, Windermere and the Lancashire fells.

Coniston Water and the Old Man of Coniston.

The Old Man of Coniston is the easiest mountain of its height (2635 feet) in the Lake District to ascend and there are rewarding prospects from the summit. These include most of Coniston Water, and, southwards, the Duddon estuary and Morecambe Bay. To the north and east one can pick out the high peaks and fells of Skiddaw, Scafell, Helvellyn and, distantly, Ingleborough and the Yorkshire fells. The lower slopes of the mountain are occasionally blemished by the scars of quarrying and of old mine workings but, taken all in all, it is a handsome mountain whose acquaintance is well worth making.

A winter view of Coniston Water and the Old Man of Coniston.

This winter photograph was taken from a point quite close to that from which the summer shot reproduced on the previous page was taken. The sprinkling of snow on the high ground and the bareness of the trees in the foreground are in marked contrast to the content of the preceding photograph.

Coniston Water from Brantwood.

Brantwood, the house in which John Ruskin lived and died, is close to the eastern shore of the lake about two miles from its head. This great Victorian writer and art authority was a fervent admirer of the Lake District and wrote with intense feeling about its great natural beauty. This is a view from the grounds of the house.

An autumn view of Tarn Hows.

Regarded by many people as the prettiest of the lakes, it is interesting to know that it is in fact an artificial lake, having been made by damming an area of marshland. It is situated a couple of miles to the north-east of Coniston. The easily gained vantage point from which the photograph was taken shows the wooded nature of the shores of the tarn and hints at the beauty of the more distant prospects, which can include the Langdale Pikes, Ill Bell and Fairfield. Another favourite viewpoint above Tarn Hows is the one from which almost the whole of Coniston Water can be seen in one direction and a panorama of fells as far north as Blencathra in the other.

Tarn Hows in Summer.

This black and white reproduction of a summer photograph shows Tarn Hows from a different angle. Clearings have been made in the foreground but the middle distance shores are well wooded, mainly with conifers. The lake's proper name is Highlow Tarn but it is now generally known as Tarn Hows, which is the name of a nearby farm.

Loweswater.

Loweswater, not much more than a mile in length, is the smallest of the chain of lakes, all of them in the Buttermere valley, comprising Buttermere, Crummock Water and Loweswater. It is about a hundred feet higher than Crummock Water, the largest lake of the three, with which it is connected by a river. Its shores, as can be seen, are nicely wooded.

Esthwaite Water.

Another of the smaller lakes, Esthwaite Water lies between Windermere and Coniston and can be reached by roads from Ambleside and from Coniston or by picking up B5285 after crossing Windermere by ferry from the Nab, near Bowness, to Ferry House. Attractive in itself, it is also close to Hawkshead, where Wordsworth was at school, and to "Hill Top", Near Sawrey, where Beatrix Potter lived and where she wrote her *Peter Rabbit* books.

Windermere at Waterhead.

As its name implies, Waterhead is at the head of Windermere and is therefore only about ten minutes walk from Ambleside, the main tourist centre for the southern part of the Lake District. There is a pier at Waterhead where passengers who have sailed up the lake can disembark from the comfortable and well equipped vessels which make the journey during the season.

Windermere and the Langdales.

The Langdale Pikes lie to the north-west of Lake Windermere and provide a magnificent back-drop to views across the lake in that direction. They are some nine or ten miles away from the point from which this early summer photograph was taken. An azalea is in bloom in the foreground of the picture.

Bow Fell and Langdale Beck.

Bow Fell, which rises to 2960 feet above sea level, is part of the high central massif that includes Scafell Pike and Scafell. Scafell Pike, at 3100 feet, is the highest summit in England. Taken in bright winter sunshine, the illustration opposite shows Bow Fell with the Little Langdale beck which eventually flows into Elterwater.

Windermere from Orrest Head.

Orrest Head is one of the favourite vantage points from which picturesque views over Windermere can be obtained. It is reached by a zig-zag path behind Windermere village and, as can be seen, an indicator chart has been installed to help visitors to locate and identify the main features of the wonderful panorama before them.

Windermere and the Langdales.

On the opposite page we reproduce yet another delightful variation on the Windermere theme. Windermere is the largest lake in the Lake District, being ten and a half miles long and up to a mile and a quarter in width. Its beauty can be enjoyed from vantage points such as the one used for this photograph, from the road along the east side of the lake or by steamer trips on the lake itself.

Windermere from Bowness.

Bowness is some two-thirds of the way up the eastern side of Lake Windermere on a little bay just below Windermere village. It is a regular intermediate stop for the passenger vessels which run throughout the season from Lakeside, at the southern end of Windermere, to Waterhead at the head of the lake. Its situation makes it accessible to many excellent viewpoints of the utmost charm and beauty and the magnificent sunset views from Bowness, so happily combining colour with silhouette, are especially notable. Belle Isle, the best known of the several islands in Lake Windermere, is almost opposite Bowness. Extending over some thirty tree-clad acres, it was bought during the eighteenth century for a Miss Isabella Curwen, after whom it was named. Small boat sailing, as the illustration suggests, is a popular pastime on Windermere and the regattas are keenly and skilfully contested.

Sailing on Lake Windermere.

Those who are fortunate enough to be able to sail on Windermere can indulge their hobby and exploit their skills in ideal conditions. The area of the lake ensures ample room for manoeuvre within a constantly changing background of trees and shrubs and bracken of many hues and varieties, with the grandeur of the fells in the distance.

Windermere from Bowness.

In the illustration on the opposite page, taken at Bowness, can be seen part of one of the pleasure craft that carry passengers on Lake Windermere between Lakeside and Waterhead via Bowness. These vessels are comfortably appointed and provide an excellent means of enjoying the varied and very real scenic beauties of the lake and its surroundings.

SWAN

Waterhead Promenade, Lake Windermere.

Sited at the northern extremity, or head, of the lake, Waterhead is best approached either by the road which follows the east side of Windermere from Bowness, or, better still, by boat, from which the grandeur and the colour of the fells beyond Ambleside can best be appreciated. Waterhead itself, on a pleasing little bay, has a water's edge promenade and a pier at which passengers cruising the lake embark and disembark.

Miller Bridge, Kendal.

Kendal is the gateway to the Lake District for visitors coming in from the south. It is a sizeable Westmorland market town on the river Kent and it is here that Flemish weavers are said to have established a woollen industry in the 14th century. Katherine Parr was born at Kendal Castle in 1512 and she may well have used the famous Queen's Room at nearby Sizergh Castle, which, with Levens Hall, are both well worth visiting while in the locality.

From the ruins of the Norman castle on an eminence just east of the town there is a fine view looking westward towards Windermere and the heights beyond. The interesting parish church dates back to the 13th century and there are several Tudor and Jacobean buildings of both historical and architectural importance to be seen in the town. Miller Bridge, forming part of the illustration opposite, is one of three stone bridges over the Kent at Kendal.

Skelwith Force.

Ambleside, near the head of Windermere, is one of the best centres for touring the Lakes. Taking the road south-west through the hamlet of Clappersgate and following the side of the lovely little river Brathay for a mile and a half will lead to Skelwith Bridge, from which a footpath soon leads to the subject of our illustration on the facing page. This sixteen foot waterfall is always a worthwhile sight whether gurgling gently or rushing headlong down as weather conditions will dictate.

Concentrated within half a day's walk of the point from which this photograph was taken is a variety of scenery that it would be difficult to match anywhere else in the Lake District. Elterwater, the exquisite Loughrigg Tarn and the charming setting of Colwith Force are examples of the pleasures in store.

Stock Ghyll Force.

Here is another attractive waterfall within easy walking distance of Ambleside. Cascading down something like 70 feet between the trees and shrubs which press in from either side, Stock Ghyll Force is an impressive sight, especially after heavy rain. Those wishing to extend their walk can continue to the Kirkstone Inn at the head of the Kirkstone Pass, admiring the splendid mass of Red Screes on the left.

It is by walking up to the many neighbouring vantage points around the town that Ambleside's ideal setting can be appreciated. Such viewpoints include Jenkyn's Crag, Loughrigg Brow and Wansfell, from each of which delightful vistas can be enjoyed.

The Old Bridge House, Ambleside.

This fascinating old building straddles the Stock beck and is used nowadays as a National Trust Tourist Information Office. Accessible from all parts of the country, Ambleside is recognised as the main tourist centre for the southern part of the Lake District. It lies beside the river Rothay with Windermere but a mile or so to its south. On the other three sides it is bounded by fells of a thousand feet or more in height, Loughrigg to the west, Wansfell to the east, Nab Scar and Fairfield to the north. The situation is therefore one that ensures that within quite a short distance of the town there are many splendid walks to be taken amidst varied, colourful and always interesting scenery.

C

Dora's Field, Rydal.

William Wordsworth's association with Grasmere preceded his move to Rydal Mount and it was at Rydal Mount that he died in 1850. This glorious bank of wild daffodils at Rydal is known as Dora's Field and cannot but bring to mind the poet's deep appreciation for and his intimate knowledge of all the natural beauty of his native Lakeland and his genius for finding words with which to clothe his thoughts.

Rydal Water.

Rydal Water, about a mile and a half north-west of Ambleside, is one of the loveliest of the smaller lakes. Its beauty is enhanced not only by a delightful setting but also by the densely wooded little islets which it contains. Rydal village, on the river Rothay, is at the east end of the lake and in the vicinity are Rydal Hall and Rydal Mount. Wordsworth lived in Rydal Mount for thirty-three years until his death in 1850. Rydal Fell, two miles to the north-west, exceeds two thousand feet in height, while in the grounds of Rydal Hall are the Rydal Falls. Very fine at all times of the year, the views are exceptionally colourful and attractive during the autumn. A mound near the lakeside, known as Wordsworth's Seat, is the one on which the poet often used to sit.

The Bridge at Rydal.

The air of softness and tranquility reflected in the facing page contrasts sharply with the stark and rugged features which dominate the scene in some other parts of the Lake District. To many people it is this remarkably wide range of scenic beauty within a comparatively small area that provides the key to its unique appeal. And nowhere could this be better demonstrated than within a very few miles of Rydal.

Wastwater, Great Gable and Lingmell.

This colourful winter composition shows part of Wastwater, Great Gable (2949 feet high) and Lingmell (2649 feet high). The lake is set in wild, stern and ruggedly mountainous country and at 258 feet it is the deepest of all the Lake District lakes. Steep scree slopes extend along much of the southern side of Wastwater, which is about three miles long.

Elterwater and the Langdales.

As it is only about three miles from Ambleside, a visit to Elterwater, one of the small lakes, can be conveniently combined with a visit to Skelwith Force and Loughrigg Tarn. The lake is about three miles in circumference and is close to the pleasing little village of the same name. There is a profusion of trees around the lake but they fortunately do not obscure this lovely view across to the Langdales which are seen standing out sharply against the skyline.

The Langdales.

Many Lakeside peaks are considerably higher than Harrison Stickle, which at 2403 feet, is the tallest of the Langdales, but the Langdale fells and valleys are nevertheless extremely attractive and are especially popular with climbers, walkers, artists and photographers.

The ascent of Harrison Stickle from Dungeon Ghyll is necessarily somewhat strenuous but the views from the top are tremendously rewarding under fair weather conditions. They include the whole extent of the Langdale Valley, with Windermere in the distance and Elterwater and Esthwaite Water at one's right. Many of the great peaks can also be identified, including Scafell, Great Gable, Bow Fell and Skiddaw. The Coniston Fells and the Helvellyn range are other notable features that are brought into view from the splendidly situated summit of Harrison Stickle.

Two views of Blea Tarn.

The black and white view of Blea Tarn, with Pike O'Stickle (2323 feet) in the distance, is almost as popular with artists and photographers as the one reproduced in colour on the opposite page. The tarn is reached from Ambleside via Skelwith Bridge, Colwith and Little Langdale, a distance of about six miles through lovely country all the way. The colourings around the tarn and among the Langdales in the background, always wonderfully rich, vary considerably through the seasons.

Cockley Beck.

Cockley Beck is the intriguing name given to one of the many little tributaries of the river Duddon. Nearby is a farm and a fell of the same name. The Duddon rises near the Three Shires Stone and steers a fascinating course from there to the sea below Duddon Bridge and Foxfield, touching Seathwaite and Ulpha on the way. The early stages of its journey are through wild and rugged country with peaks in excess of two thousand feet on either side but below Cockley Beck the river, after passing through the gorges at Birks Bridge and Wallowbarrow, reaches Seathwaite, after which its valley widens and the fells become lower and altogether less severe. In its course of about fourteen miles the Duddon drops something like two thousand feet through scenery of an almost endless variety.

Grasmere Church.

St. Oswald's church at Grasmere, with its splendid 14th century tower, is the burial place of two of the literary giants whose names are inseparably linked with the Lake District. They are William Wordsworth and Hartley Coleridge. The church is the scene of a delightful annual rush-bearing festival on the Saturday nearest St. Oswald's Day in August.

Grasmere from Dale End.

Dale End is at the southern end of Grasmere and the view on the facing page looks right across to Grasmere village on the northern side of the lake. Grasmere and Rydal Water are linked by the river Rothay and each is embellished by charming tree-clad islets. The woods on the western bank of Grasmere are notable and the setting as a whole has very considerable charm.

Grasmere.

It has been possible in this photograph to include most of the surface area of this small but very attractive lake. Grasmere is about a mile in length and some half a mile wide with a maximum depth of about a hundred and eighty feet. The slopes to the surrounding fells are gentler and the scenery in the immediate vicinity of the lake is softer than is usual in the Lake District as a whole.

Grasmere from Wishing Gate.

The Wishing Gate viewpoint features the bracken and tree clad foreground, the islet, the slopes that climb away from the distant shore and the fells to which they eventually lead. Wishing Gate is but one of a number of splendid vantage points from which memorable vistas of the lake and the surrounding countryside can be obtained and at every turn some new and moving splendour will appear, captivating the eye and stimulating the imagination.

Dove Cottage, Grasmere.

William Wordsworth lived in Dove Cottage from 1799 until 1808. Coleridge and De Quincey also lived in Grasmere and the De Quinceys lived at Dove Cottage for a time after Wordsworth had left it for Rydal Mount. Dove Cottage is open to the public at advertised times and contains many interesting Wordsworth relics and mementos, including a fine collection of manuscripts.

Brothers Water.

A592, on its way from Patterdale towards the Kirkstone Pass, runs along the east side of Brothers Water, a small and altogether charming lake which is linked with Ullswater by the Goldrill Beck and the Patterdale valley. High peaks abound. Those to the west include Fairfield, Helvellyn and Dollywaggon Pike, with Kidsty Pike and The Knott to the east and all of them within a radius of less than five miles.

Thirlmere.

It is difficult, looking at the illustration on the facing page, to believe that Thirlmere is in fact a Manchester Corporation reservoir, supplying fifty million gallons of water a day through a pipeline a hundred miles long. The lake is more than three miles in length and is some five hundred feet above sea level. The route from Grasmere, along A591, northward to Thirlmere follows first the river Rothay and then the Raise Beck and after breasting Dunmail Raise the lake comes into view. By taking the minor road on the west side, which passes below Brown Rigg, Armboth Fell, High Seat and Raven Crag, it is possible to secure a succession of magnificent views over and beyond the tree-clad lakeside. Thirlmere, reservoir though it may be, remains one of the loveliest of all our English lakes.

Another view of Thirlmere.

This second view of Thirlmere looks more along the length of the lake. Its water level was raised by fifty feet when it was taken over for use as a reservoir, but, as can be seen, it does not appear to have been achieved at the expense of the lake's natural attractiveness. The visitor's room for manoeuvre away from the road along the western side may still be somewhat restricted but nothing can detract from the varied beauties of the views eastward, which include a splendid sight of Helvellyn which, at 3118 feet, is the third tallest of all the Lakeland peaks. Thirlmere is about equidistant between Keswick and Grasmere.

The Kirkstone Pass.

The Kirkstone Pass is an exciting feature on A592, the main road which connects Ullswater with Windermere. At fourteen hundred and seventy six feet above sea level it is by no means the highest of the Lake District passes but it offers some outstandingly attractive views. In the illustration on the opposite page Brothers Water is seen almost a thousand feet below the point from which the photograph was taken. In the opposite direction, facing southwards, there are vantage points in the pass from which superb views of much of the length of Lake Windermere are obtainable. The fells rise steeply to peaks of more than two thousand feet on either side of the pass and the interplay of sunshine and shadow can produce some truly remarkable effects through a seemingly limitless variety of changing colour values.

Newby Bridge.

Newby Bridge is a hamlet which lies barely a mile south of the foot of Lake Windermere. It is on the river Leven which flows out of the lake to start its journey to the sea at Morecambe Bay and the old bridge itself is of an interesting and unusual design. Situated amidst delightful surroundings, characterized by woods and plantations in an undulating countryside, Newby Bridge is easily reached from Grange-over-Sands along A590, from Windermere town by A592, which runs along the east side of the lake, or by A590 if approaching from Barrow-in-Furness, Ulverston and the west. There is some excellent hotel accommodation and visitors can fish and boat peacefully in what makes a good place to stop before moving on again to the pleasures in store to the north.

Ullswater.

More than seven miles long and second in size only to Windermere, Ullswater ranks high by any reckoning so far as the scenic beauty of its setting is concerned. The most north-easterly of the lakes, it is barely six miles from Penrith, the northern gateway to Lakeland. Ullswater is made up of three zig-zag reaches of which the first, starting from Patterdale, runs almost due north, the second is mainly easterly and the third heads north-east to terminate at Pooley Bridge, from whose pier during the season a motor yacht service runs the full length of the lake, with stops at Howtown and Glenridding. Small boat sailing on the lake is very popular but care must be taken to be ready for the sudden squalls that can blow up on account of the configuration of the surrounding hills.

Striding Edge, Helvellyn.

Comfortably topping the three thousand foot mark, Helvellyn dominates the mass of heights which rise steeply behind Glenridding at the southern end of Ullswater to separate Ullswater from Thirlmere. The narrow, rocky ledge known as Striding Edge, illustrated here, is part of one of the three generally recognised routes up this very handsome mountain.

Ullswater from Gowbarrow.

Gowbarrow is on the northern side of the middle reach of Ullswater and it was here that Wordsworth wrote his immortal *Ode to the Daffodils*. He had close family associations with the Ullswater area and this was his favourite lake. The summit of Gowborrow Fell is less than sixteen hundred feet above sea level but the views to the north, south and east are exceptionally fine. Now National Trust property, the Fell extends over more than seven hundred acres.

Daffodils at Ullswater.

It may well have been daffodils in a similar situation to this that gave Wordsworth his inspiration in 1804. In addition to his verse, he wrote glowingly in prose of the delights of the Ullswater countryside of which he had such an intimate and enthusiastic personal knowledge.

Ullswater from Gowbarrow Park.

The views from the lakeside around Gowbarrow offer a variety of prospects which are made more interesting and more colourful by reason of the fact that along this stretch of Ullswater the scenery has become bolder than was the case at the Pooley Bridge, or northern, extremity of the lake and this makes it possible for a great deal of its beauty to be enjoyed without the necessity for ascending very far from the water's edge.

Aira Force.

Aira Force lies just behind the junction of A5091, which comes down from Troutbeck, with A592 which follows the northern shore of Ullswater. The falls are within the Gowbarrow National Trust Park and are a lovely sight as they cascade some seventy feet over the rocks in a cool and beautiful woodland setting. Other delightful waterfalls that can be seen in the Lake District include Scale Force, about two miles west of Buttermere village, which has a drop of one hundred and twenty four feet, Lodore Falls, near the foot of Derwentwater, which leaps over ninety feet, Stock Ghyll Force, near Ambleside, and Dungeon Ghyll at Elterwater, both of which fall sixty feet or more.

Ullswater.

This view of Ullswater was taken from near to Martindale and looks towards the lower lying country at the northern end of the lake. The walk from Howtown pier, near Martindale, to Patterdale, a distance of about six miles along the shore of the lake, is one that shows Ullswater at its best.

The Head of Ullswater.

The colour reproduction opposite is of the head of Ullswater and features the gentler contours of the wooded slopes which characterise that locality. Every one of the lakes has its own fervent admirers, sometimes to the exclusion of all others, but to most visitors to the Lake District the tremendously varied beauty of Ullswater will always rank high in their recollections.

The Bowder Stone, Borrowdale.

Borrowdale is the name given to the beautiful valley of the river Derwent which flows north into Derwentwater. The lush green of the banks of the river contrasts vividly with the varied colourings of the fells which rise sharply up on either side. The Bowder Stone, estimated to weigh two thousand tons, is just to the east of the main road between the villages of Grange and Rosthwaite.

Ullswater.

This last look at Ullswater endeavours to summarize its outstanding characteristics. These include its zig-zag course and its varied but frequently tree clad shores from which high fells can often be seen to rise and climb impressively towards the skyline. This is ideal walking country but a splendid alternative is to sail the length of the lake by passenger launch. It is a memorable experience.

Watendlath Tarn.

Watendlath tarn and village make a popular excursion for visitors to Keswick, five miles away. They are a couple of miles south of the foot of Derwentwater and are separated from Borrowdale by Grange Fell. Sir Hugh Walpole, the author of the *Rogue Herries* series of novels, made Watendlath the home of Judith Paris.

Ashness Bridge.

This is an autumn photograph of the very famous view which shows Ashness Bridge, part of Derwentwater and, beyond it, Skiddaw (3053 feet). The bridge is reached by a turning at Barrow Landing off the Keswick to Borrowdale road, which runs along the eastern bank of Derwentwater. A visit to Ashness Bridge is usually combined with a visit to Watendlath as they are less than three miles apart.

Watendlath Bridge.

At the foot of Watendlath Tarn is this lovely old pack-horse bridge. The views in the vicinity are notable, especially from the high ground between Watendlath and Rosthwaite in Borrowdale. A walk in the opposite direction, towards Armboth, yielding splendid prospects of Thirlmere, also has much to commend it.

Derwentwater and Causey Pike.

Comfortably topping the two thousand feet contour, Causey Pike lies four miles west of Keswick. The promontory in the foreground of the picture opposite is known as Friar's Crag and from it visitors can enjoy some of the finest scenery in the district. Two other magnificent vantage points in the immediate vicinity of Keswick are those at Latrigg and Castle Head.

Derwentwater from Castle Head.

This is a view that was mentioned in the previous caption. Derwentwater is approximately three miles by a mile and a quarter and most of it can be seen from Castle Head, the view including Lord's, Derwent and St. Herbert's islands. Although only some five hundred feet above sea level, Castle Head yields splendid panoramas the details of which can be identified from the plan which is shown in the foreground of the black and white photograph.

Derwentwater from Latrigg.

Latrigg, at twelve hundred feet, overlooks Keswick and Derwentwater and provides a viewpoint from which a large expanse of the distant fells can easily be seen, as can the splendid peaks of Blencathra (2847 feet) to the north-east and Helvellyn (3118 feet) to the south-east.

Derwentwater from Surprise View.

Taken from the Borrowdale end of Derwentwater, this view looks north over the lake's little islets and on towards Keswick and the fells beyond. The actual viewpoint is close to Ashness Woods which steeply overlook the Keswick to Borrowdale road.

The Honister Pass.

The Honister Pass is on B5289 which links Borrowdale and Seatoller with Buttermere. The road climbs steeply from Seatoller to the highest point of the pass, which is almost twelve hundred feet above sea level, before dropping, less steeply, some eight hundred feet along the side of Gatesgarth Beck to Buttermere and Buttermere village. Honister Crags and Fleetwith Pike (2126 feet) almost overlook the road on the left with Yew Crag and Dale Head (2473 feet) matching them on the right.

Derwentwater and Castlerigg Fell.

A clearing above the trees near the south-west corner of Derwentwater makes for a peaceful and pleasing composition of woods and water, fell and sky in the nicely balanced proportions that can be readily appreciated even in a black and white reproduction.

Derwentwater and Blencathra.

Looking towards the north-east with the massive pile of Blencathra, or Saddleback, as it is also known, in the background, this is one of the classic views of Derwentwater. By its very nature it is a view that is certain to be of interest at all seasons of the year and it is one that makes the ascent to this vantage point, in the vicinity of Cat Bells, which rises to 1480 feet, very well worth while.

Derwentwater and Bassenthwaite.

By ascending the high ground in the direction of High Seat, to the south-east of Derwentwater, and not far from Watendlath, one is rewarded with a splendid panorama that includes parts of both Derwentwater and Bassenthwaite with the lofty Skiddaw Fells to the right. The two lakes, about three miles apart, are linked by the river Derwent.

Friar's Crag, Derwentwater.

A very short walk along a path from the little landing stage at the Keswick end of Derwentwater brings one to the pine-clad rocky eminence known as Friar's Crag. The name is said to associate the spot with landings made long ago by Furness friars journeying from Borrowdale to Keswick. Derwent Isle is situated almost opposite to Friar's Crag and both are now part of the property of the National Trust.

Bassenthwaite Lake and Skiddaw.

Small boat sailing is obviously popular on Bassenthwaite Lake, which is about four miles in length. A594 travels the well-wooded western side of the lake and frequently runs close to the shore. A591, on the opposite side, keeps further away at all times but there are several footpath accesses to the lake from the road while in the opposite direction the mass of Skiddaw reaches up to an impressive summit height of more than three thousand feet.

Buttermere.

Approached from Borrowdale over the Honister Pass (B5289), Buttermere is the first of a fine trio of lakes. The others are Crummock Water and Loweswater, the last named being the smallest at barely a mile in length. Buttermere is something over one mile long while Crummock Water's length is two and a half. The motor road keeps to the right of Buttermere but there is a fine walk, partly through National Trust woods, along the opposite side.

Buttermere Village.

The little village of Buttermere is surrounded by exciting country and lies mid way between the lake of the same name and Crummock Water. It makes a fine base for an exhilarating choice of easy, moderate and strenuous walks beside and beyond its two neighbouring lakes. Even in this black and white photograph there is a suggestion of the important part that is played by light and shade effects in this locality.

Fleetwith and Buttermere.

Fleetwith can here be seen rising two thousand one hundred and twenty six feet above the Honister Crags that shield the sides which face out towards Buttermere. Buttermere is surrounded by a ring of magnificent high fells with many peaks exceeding the height of Fleetwith Pike so that the views, in good weather, from almost any one of them are of considerable beauty and grandeur.

Crummock Water.

This black and white study of Crummock Water reveals surroundings of a gentler nature, in contrast to the rather bolder characteristics which are reproduced on page 95. It is the very fact that the scene can change so quickly that makes the Crummock Water area especially popular with artists and photographers, particularly as there are so many easily reached vantage points for them to use.

Another aspect of Buttermere.

Here is another example of the changes being rung by sunshine and shadow at Buttermere where, for some distance from either end of the lake, the ground is little higher above sea level than the lake itself but where, from the other two sides the rising fells, in contrast, reach up another two thousand feet in little more than a mile on the map. It is because of these configurations that the sun and the clouds can weave the fascinating and endlessly varied patterns that captivate the eye of the beholder.

Melbreak and Crummock Water.

Crummock Water and Melbreak are in an area of moods and contrasts. This, of course, is equally true of many other areas and for this reason they make a suitable subject for the last illustration in this Lake District publication. While Melbreak achieves less than half the height of Lakeland's highest peaks it is certainly not without character as it stands guard over the north-west corner of the lake. It is moderately easy to climb and is best approached from the south along the Scale Beck footpath before swinging right to the slopes which rise to Melbreak's table-like top. Scale Force, with a drop of a hundred and twenty feet, which makes it England's highest waterfall, lies a little farther up the beck and the short diversion required to reach it should certainly be made. The National Trust is responsible for the care and preservation of Crummock Water as a place of natural beauty and it was through the Trust's initiative that great improvements have been made at Lanthwaite Wood where pine and oak are being planted to replace the stunted beech trees.

Index to Illustrations